DIVINE DOG TREATS

Recipes for a Happy, Healthy Pet

WENDY LIOU

iUniverse, Inc.
New York   Bloomington

Divine Dog Treats
Recipes for a Happy, Healthy Pet

iUniverse books may be ordered through booksellers or by contacting:

iUniverse
1663 Liberty Drive
Bloomington, IN 47403
www.iuniverse.com
1-800-Authors (1-800-288-4677)

Because of the dynamic nature of the Internet, any Web addresses or
links contained in this book may have changed since publication and
may no longer be valid. The views expressed in this work are solely those
of the author and do not necessarily reflect the views of the publisher,
and the publisher hereby disclaims any responsibility for them.

ISBN: 978-1-4502-4560-9 (sc)
ISBN: 978-1-4502-4561-6 (ebook)

Library of Congress Control Number: 2010932796

Printed in the United States of America

iUniverse rev. date: 07/29/2010

To my beloved, Meg:

You are my best friend, motivation, inspiration, and teacher. It is a true gift to experience your unconditional love. Thank you for showing me how to open up to all possibilities. You are a blessing beyond boundaries and joy without limits. I honor you, respect you, and love you!

Meg & Me

"I have two dogs; one is picky and the other is not. My picky toy poodle didn't sniff twice. My dogs enjoy these treats. It's good to know that I am giving them something that is good for them and made without all the preservatives, artificial colorings, and by-products that are in some commercially made treats." Dr. K. Blackwell, DVM, Phoenix, Ariz.

"Our pug is extremely fussy and breaks out from every store-bought treat. He loves these treats and has never broken out from any of them. These treats are delicious and satisfying. The recipes are created straight from the heart of someone who really cares about pets." Tanya, Canton, Mich.

"My dogs love the treats! I also like the fact that they are natural with no salt or additives. I would recommend them to all my pet parents." Sue, Peoria, Ariz. (counselor and author of *Because of Sean*, www.auraimages.com)

"My pugs love Divine Dog Treats. These are by far the healthiest, freshest, and now favorite snacks for my little ones." Bobbie, Phoenix, Ariz.

"Being in the health industry, it is important to me to make sure my dogs are ingesting the most healthful ingredients. With *Divine Dog Treats* you know exactly what is in each treat because you're making it from scratch. Nothing is more comforting than using these creative and easy-to-follow recipes to make healthy, palatable treats for my precious puppies." Courtney, Avondale, Ariz.

Contents

INTRODUCTION

It is with great enthusiasm that I say to you, "Congratulations for investing in your pet's health!" Baking your own treats, with *zero* preservatives, can give you peace of mind knowing you are providing the best for your animal companion(s). Treats are also a fun way to spice up your pet's diet! Due to the lack of preservatives in the treats you are about to make, it is necessary to refrigerate or freeze them to assure freshness and tastiness.

The recipes in this book are a healthy alternative to many store-bought snacks and combine the palatability to discerning noses that you, the proud pet-parent are looking for. However, treats should only be 10 percent of your dog's regular intake. Remember to have lots of fun with the whole baking process!

I am often asked how I got started making dog treats. I love to bake healthy muffins and cookies. Therefore, when Meg came into my life, it was natural for me to begin experimenting with something else. I want her to be as healthy as possible and to have a long life. The only way I know how is to provide exercise, quality food, and healthy treats without preservatives and artificial ingredients. Once I realized that what I wanted was not readily available, I got creative. The rest, shall we say, is doggone history.

Important to note: I have eaten and sampled all the treats, as have many of my friends before they gave them to their dogs. These treats are fit for human consumption and are healthy too!

HOW WE MET

It is 2003 and for about a year I contemplated getting a dog. One day, when shopping, I randomly came upon a boy with a dog. This little dog was so cute and friendly.

As I was petting the dog, the boy said something to the effect: "I think the breeders are going to have more puppies. Do you want their number?"

I said yes without hesitation. I walked away and suddenly stopped in my tracks. I had to call *right now*. I cannot explain it, but I dialed the number at that moment. After twenty minutes on the phone, to my surprise, I had my name on the list for a puppy!

It really hit me that I had not cared for anything else before, and this was a big commitment. Months later, I was jumping out of my skin because I still had not heard from the breeders. The day I called to follow up, the litter had just been born a few hours earlier. Since my name was first on the list, I was able to pick my puppy first. I really wanted a girl. Of the three dogs born, there was only one girl. She was *the one*. Still is to this day.

After seven years, I never get tired of telling that story. Baking healthy treats is one way I tell Meg every day that I love her and her actions show me the love back.

In my opinion, dogs are amazing animals and have great gifts to offer us. If you bought this book, you know exactly what I mean. I hope these recipes bring as much joy to your life and increase the bond you and your dog have as they have done for mine.

BAKING TIPS

For all recipes, I baked the treats in the middle oven rack with baking temperatures and times from my oven. The size of the treat you make can also modify the suggested baking time (the larger the size, the longer the baking might take).

Check treats often (especially the first time you make them) to avoid burning. Please use the notes pages to document baking times with your oven, as there may be variances. Always, always, always cool treats before serving to avoid burning your doggie's mouth.

Kitchen basics to have handy include

- Cookie sheet (I suggest the type with the air circulating on the bottom)
- Wax paper for rolling out treats and parchment paper for the bottom of your cookie sheet during baking if you don't want to grease or spray your cookie sheet
- Non-stick rolling pin (I suggest silicone instead of the wooden type)
- Cookie cutters in the appropriate size for your pet
- Measuring cups and spoons
- Large metal or glass bowl

Definitions of kitchen terms used in this book

- Tbsp = tablespoon
- tsp = teaspoon
- C = cup
- approx. = approximately

ADDITIONAL BAKING TIPS

1. Completely cool treats and store in air-tight containers either in the refrigerator or freezer. If you freeze treats, always thaw prior to serving to your pet.
2. Most of the ingredients listed in the recipes may have an organic version, if available. Purchase whatever you feel the most comfortable using.
3. When a recipe calls for water, you can use bottled, purified, distilled, or tap.
4. When you roll out the dough and cut into shapes, be sure to combine the scraps of dough and roll it out again until all the dough is used.
5. Some cookie sheets can be made as non-stick. If you are using a non-stick cookie sheet, you don't have to grease it. Also, instead of greasing the cookie sheet, parchment paper does very nicely at keeping your treats from sticking to the pan.
6. Some treats have a higher moisture content due to more water or fruit in them. If a recipe asks you to leave treats in your cooling oven, this is to make them a crispier or harder biscuit.
7. A cooling oven refers the oven after you've turned it off.
8. Disclaimer: The information provided in this book is not intended to diagnose or treat illness or disease. If your dog has a known allergy or is on a restricted diet, do not make that particular recipe or consult your veterinarian. Also, consult your veterinarian for treatment, diagnosis, or meal plans specific to your animal's needs.

Recipe for a Divinely Happy Dog
(a poem from the author)

All of these ingredients are easy to get.
They come from your heart, so please do not forget—
to reward your furry friend with a treat every day.
A Divinely Happy Dog will be yours with no delay!

Ingredients:
1 cup of Love
½ cup of Exercise
¼ cup of Discipline
1 Tbsp of Respect
1 tsp of Patience

Directions:
1. Love is the main ingredient your pet gives you unconditionally. So give a hearty dose back and you will both be exceptionally happy!
2. Added next is a lively dose of exercise. This reduces boredom and keeps your favorite shoes from meeting an untimely demise.
3. Next, mix in discipline and set limitations. It keeps harmonious order without any frustrations.
4. Every dog has certain instincts, this you should expect. So research your breed and give it the utmost respect.
5. Last, add patience. This we sometimes forget to do. For your animal mirrors your feelings and shines them back at you.
6. When all the ingredients balance just right, a Divinely Happy Dog will be yours day and night.

CHAPTER 1

SPECIAL OCCASION TREATS

My present is in here!

BIRTHDAY CAKE COOKIE

Okay, sing along: "Happy Birthday to (your dog's name)!" This treat is absolutely perfect for that special birthday party! If you are planning a party, double the recipe to be sure every four-legged guest takes home a doggie-bag of fresh treats! Single batch makes approx. 2–2 ½ dozen.

Ingredients:
1 C unbleached, white flour
1 Tbsp white sugar
1 Tbsp canola oil
½ tsp pure vanilla extract
⅓ C water

Directions:
1. Preheat oven to 350°.
2. In a bowl, combine flour and sugar.
3. Add water, oil, and vanilla. Mix with a large spoon.
4. When dough starts to get crumbly, by hand, knead dough until it sticks together.
5. Roll dough out on wax paper or floured surface. Cut into 1 ½-inch-sized bones. Note: baking time will vary if your shape is smaller or larger.
6. Bake 20–30 minutes or until bottoms are lightly browned. Start checking treats at the 20 minute mark. Once lightly browned, turn off oven and put treats back in cooling oven for an additional 10–15 minutes to harden.

This Valentine Vittle is my heart's desire!

VALENTINE VITTLE

Put a little love in the air with this sweet cinnamon treat. Make this one in a heart shape to show your furry friend(s) how much you care this Valentine's Day or *any* day of the week! Makes approx. 3 ½–4 dozen.

Ingredients:
1 ¼ C wheat flour (plus extra for flouring rollout surface)
½ C wheat germ
¼ C ground flax meal
1 tsp cinnamon
¼ C honey
4–6 Tbsp water, divided into 4 Tbsp and 2 Tbsp

Directions:
1. Preheat oven to 350°.
2. Mix the first four dry ingredients well in a large bowl.
3. Add honey and 4 Tbsp water and mix together.
4. Add additional water if mixture is not holding completely together.
5. By hand, knead dough into a ball.
6. On wax paper or a floured surface, roll dough out to ¼-inch thickness and cut into heart (or your favorite) shape.
7. Bake for 20–25 minutes or until bottoms are browned.

Little Gobblers- Turkey Day Treat

TURKEY DAY TREAT

This is a scrumptious way to show your gratitude to the furry friends in your life. A wonderful idea is to package some of these treats in festive baggies. When dinner guests are taking leftovers home, hand them some homemade treats for their doggies too! Makes approx. 3–4 dozen.

Ingredients:
1 C wheat flour
¼ C cornmeal
⅛ tsp poultry seasoning
½ tsp parsley flakes
1 Tbsp vegetable oil
1 Tbsp water
4-ounce jar organic turkey and vegetable baby food

Directions:
1. Preheat oven to 325°.
2. Blend flour, cornmeal, and seasonings well.
3. Add baby food, oil, and water until dough clumps up. Then knead by hand to prepare rolling dough out.
4. Roll out on a lightly floured surface and cut into your favorite shape.
5. Bake on a non-stick cookie sheet for 30–35 minutes or until golden brown.

Nothing spooky about these tasty treats —Pumpkin Patch

PUMPKIN PATCH

This is a spinoff of the Halloween Harvest treat. Try this if you don't have a ripe banana on hand and still want to bake up a festive Halloween treat. Please note some of the ingredient amounts changed from the original recipe, but it's just as lip-smacking good as the first version! Makes approx. 3 dozen.

Ingredients:
½ C canned pumpkin
1 C uncooked oatmeal
⅓ C wheat flour
¼ C ground flax meal
½ tsp *each* cinnamon and nutmeg
1 Tbsp vegetable oil

Directions:
1. Preheat oven to 350°.
2. Mix pumpkin, flax, cinnamon, and nutmeg together.
3. Add oatmeal and wheat flour, mix well.
4. Blend in vegetable oil.
5. On a floured surface or wax paper, roll dough out to ¼-inch thickness and cut into your favorite Halloween shape.
6. Bake for 20 minutes or until bottoms are lightly browned. Once lightly browned, turn off oven and place treats back into cooling oven for 20–25 minutes to harden.

HALLOWEEN HARVEST

Pumpkins are one of many symbols for Halloween. Why not have it in a dog treat? The touch of cinnamon and nutmeg make the kitchen smell like a fresh pumpkin pie is in the oven. Be sure to have these on hand just in case you get some furry, four-legged trick-or-treaters! Makes approx. 4 dozen.

Ingredients:
1 ripe banana (6–7 inches long)
½ C canned pumpkin
1 C uncooked oatmeal
1 ¼ C wheat flour, divided into ¾ C and ½ C
⅓ C ground flax meal
½ tsp *each* cinnamon and nutmeg
2 Tbsp water

Directions:
1. Preheat oven to 400°.
2. Peel and mash banana.
3. Add pumpkin and blend together.
4. Mix in cinnamon, nutmeg, and ground flax.
5. Add oatmeal and ¾ cup wheat flour, mix well.
6. Blend in water.
7. Knead in remaining ½ cup of wheat flour a few tablespoons at a time. Let sit for 10 minutes in bowl.
8. On wax paper or floured surface, roll dough out to ¼-inch thickness and cut into your favorite Halloween shape.
9. Bake for 10–13 minutes or until bottoms are lightly browned. Once lightly browned, turn off oven and place treats back into cooling oven for 20–25 minutes to harden.

CHOMPIN' CHRISTMAS COOKIE

'Tis the season to be baking, so please include your canine companion too! These treats are a perfect gift to bring to a holiday party, if the host/hostess is a dog lover like you. Purchase a fun dog bowl and fill with these fabulous, homemade treats. Just be sure to tell the recipient that these treats have no preservatives, so refrigeration is necessary to preserve quality. Makes approx. 2 dozen.

Ingredients:
½ C wheat flour
½ C unbleached, white flour
1 tsp ground ginger
½ tsp cinnamon
2 Tbsp honey
3–6 Tbsp water, divided in half

Directions:
1. Preheat oven to 350°.
2. Mix flour, ginger, and cinnamon until spices are evenly distributed.
3. Add honey and 2 Tbsp water. Mix until dough becomes crumbly.
4. Knead by hand into a ball. If dough is not holding together, add additional water 1 tablespoon at a time. If you added too much water, add more flour to balance out.
5. Roll dough out on wax paper or floured surface. Cut into your favorite holiday shape (like a gingerbread man).
6. Bake for 15–20 minutes or until bottoms are browned.

Are these for me or Santa?
Chompin' Christmas Cookies

Baking Notes:

CHAPTER 2

HEALTH & WELLNESS TREATS

Exercise smells like fun!

HEALTHY, HAPPY HEART

The ingredients in this treat all have protective properties for the heart: vitamin E, omega-3 fatty acids, monounsaturated and polyunsaturated fats, phytochemicals, fiber, and trace minerals such as iron, selenium, calcium, magnesium, and folate. With a list of healthy ingredients like that, the store-bought dog treats pale in comparison! Make your dog's heart a happy one! Makes approx. 2 ½ dozen.

Ingredients:
24 unsalted whole almonds
¼ C sunflower seeds
½ C ground flax meal
½ C oat bran
2 Tbsp honey
⅓ C water
⅓ C whole wheat flour

Directions:
1. Preheat oven to 325°.
2. Place almonds and sunflower seeds in a food processor for 1 minute or until nuts are ground up to a coarse flour consistency.
3. Blend nut mixture, ground flax, and oat bran together.
4. Add water and honey. Mix well.
5. Knead in wheat flour a little at a time to form a ball.
6. Roll out on wax paper and cut into your pet's favorite treat shape.
7. Bake for 15 minutes or until bottoms are browned. Once lightly browned, turn off oven and place treats back into cooling oven for 10–15 minutes to harden.

Apple Cider Cookies

APPLE CIDER COOKIES

Apple cider vinegar has a long history of testimonials and folklore surrounding its benefits. The *best* apple cider vinegar is the raw, unfiltered, organic kind so it retains the natural enzymes, minerals, and nutrients. Some possible ways apple cider vinegar may assist the body are in removing toxins, soothing irritated skin, improving digestion, and supporting the immune system. Once you make this treat, you are sure to have your faithful friend coming back for seconds! Makes approx. 3 dozen.

Ingredients:
½ C uncooked oatmeal
¾ C wheat flour, divided into ½ C and ¼ C
½ tsp cinnamon
3 Tbsp apple cider vinegar (raw, unfiltered, organic)
1 Tbsp vegetable/canola oil
3 Tbsp honey

Directions:
1. Preheat oven to 325°.
2. Blend oatmeal, ½ cup of the flour, and cinnamon.
3. In a separate bowl, combine the oil, honey, and vinegar until the honey dissolves.
4. Add the vinegar mixture to the oatmeal/flour/cinnamon bowl and blend well.
5. Add remaining ¼ cup flour and work in by hand to form a ball ready for rolling out.
6. On wax paper, roll out dough and cut into 1-inch circles (or your favorite treat shape) until all dough is used. You may need to add a pinch of flour when rolling out to avoid dough sticking to the surface.
7. Bake for 15–20 minutes or until bottoms are lightly browned.

Let me see what smells so tasty!
Diabetic Delight Treat

DIABETIC DELIGHT

Diabetes can be a challenging disease for a dog. The pet owner has a responsibility to monitor blood sugar levels, plan meals, and provide plenty of exercise. Some veterinarians recommend a higher fiber diet. High fiber in your pet's diet can aid in stabilizing blood sugar levels as well as providing food and snacks with a balance of protein, fat, and carbohydrates. This treat is just what the veterinarian ordered! Makes approx. 3 ½ dozen.

Ingredients:
½ C unsalted, sunflower seeds
½ C garbanzo bean flour (also known as chickpeas)
1 C uncooked oatmeal
2 Tbsp canola oil
1 egg white
¼ C water
½ tsp cinnamon

Directions:
1. Preheat oven to 325°.
2. Place sunflower seeds in a food processor for 1 minute or until nuts are ground to a coarse flour consistency.
3. Mix together well the sunflower seeds, garbanzo bean flour, oatmeal, and cinnamon.
4. Add water, egg white, and oil and blend together.
5. Knead dough into a ball. Note: the longer you knead and work with the dough, the less sticky it will be as the oats will absorb some of the water and make it easier to roll out to cut into treats.
6. Roll out on wax paper and cut into your pet's favorite treat shape.
7. Bake for 20–30 minutes or until bottoms are golden brown.

I can't wait much longer for my Gluten Free Goodie!

GLUTEN FREE GOODIES

Wheat and gluten sensitivity is an allergy that affects certain dogs. Keeping a keen eye on the food's ingredient list is a heavy responsibility for the pet owner. These heavenly treats are formulated especially for the wheat/gluten-sensitive dog. However, *all* dogs can appreciate the out-of-this-world terrific taste! Makes approx. 3 dozen.

Ingredients:
½ C brown rice flour, divided in half
½ C almond meal
½ C ground flax meal
¼ C water
1 egg white

Directions:
1. Preheat oven to 350°.
2. Blend ¼ cup of the rice flour, flax meal, and almond meal together.
3. Mix in water and egg white.
4. Add last ¼ cup of rice flour when kneading dough by hand.
5. Roll out dough between two pieces of wax paper to prevent dough from sticking to the rolling pin and cut into your dogs favorite treat shape.
6. Bake for 20–25 minutes or until bottoms are browned and treats are hard to the touch.

CHOLESTEROL BUSTER BONES

High cholesterol is not just a problem for humans. Pets can have high cholesterol too, especially if table scraps are often given. Try this ultra-healthy treat! Don't forget to include plenty of exercise to lower that cholesterol (yours and your pet's), too! Makes approx. 6 dozen.

Ingredients:
2 C oat bran
1 C uncooked oatmeal
1 C canned pumpkin
2–4 Tbsp water
3 Tbsp canola oil
½ tsp cinnamon

Directions:
1. Preheat oven to 350°.
2. Blend pumpkin, cinnamon, and oil in a large bowl.
3. Add all the oat bran and mix until crumbly.
4. Add oatmeal in by hand, approximately ¼ cup at a time.
5. Add 2–4 tablespoons of water for the final binding of the oatmeal.
6. Knead dough for several minutes. You may need to break dough in half to get a better handle on kneading since this is a large batch.
7. Roll out on wax paper, cut into your favorite treat shape.
8. Bake for 30–40 minutes or until bottoms are browned and treats are hard to the touch.

LOW-FAT FAVORITES

Our furry friends can pack on a weight problem for a variety of reasons. Low-fat treats can provide your pet with a super tasty snack without going overboard on calories. With that in mind, these treats have less than a half gram of fat per one treat serving. Makes approx. 3 ½ dozen.

Ingredients:
½ C unsweetened applesauce
½ tsp nutmeg
¼ C ground flax meal
2 C uncooked oatmeal
¼ C water
Approx. 2 Tbsp of flour for treat roll/cut out

Directions:
1. Preheat oven to 350°.
2. Mix together applesauce and nutmeg until evenly distributed.
3. Add flax meal and blend.
4. Mix in all 2 cups of the oats until crumbly.
5. Add the water, blend, then form a ball (note: it will be sticky to the touch).
6. Dust a sheet of wax paper with flour. Put about ½ tablespoon of flour in your hands and coat the ball of dough.
7. Roll out and cut into favorite treat shape.
8. Bake for 20–25 minutes or until bottoms of treats are lightly browned. Once bottoms are browned, turn off oven and place treats back in cooling oven for 20–30 minutes for treats to harden.

Heavenly treats to help your dog's tummy.
Upset Tummy Treat

UPSET TUMMY TREATS

Calming ginger and soothing cinnamon will help ease the stomach *before* your faithful friend encounters any nervous circumstances (like riding in the car, going to the vet or groomer, or traveling). Keep these on hand and treat your pet before your planned stressful situation. Makes approx. 4 dozen.

Ingredients:
4 inches of a ripe banana (about half a banana)
¼ C unsweetened applesauce
1 C brown rice flour, divided in half
½ C uncooked oatmeal
1 ½ tsp ground ginger
½ tsp cinnamon

Directions:
1. Preheat oven to 375°.
2. Peel and mash banana then mix in applesauce.
3. Blend in ginger and cinnamon.
4. Add oats and ½ cup of the rice flour and mix well.
5. Knead in by hand the other ½ cup of the rice flour until the dough is no longer very sticky. Form dough into a ball, wash hands, and roll dough out on wax paper. Cut into favorite treat shape.
6. Bake for 15–20 minutes or until treats are browned and hard.

Baking Notes:

CHAPTER 3

FRUIT-TASTIC TREATS

My mouth waters for these treats!

RISE & SHINE SNACKS

Make your pet happy before you leave for work and serve up this mouth-watering morsel. With healthy carbs and fiber, your pal will stay satisfied all day until you come home for dinner. Makes approx. 2 dozen.

Ingredients:
2 Tbsp creamy, unsalted peanut butter
2 Tbsp unsweetened applesauce
1 Tbsp ground flax meal
1 ¼ C uncooked oatmeal
2 Tbsp honey
2 Tbsp water, divided in half

Directions:
1. Preheat oven to 325° (see step #8 as well).
2. Blend together peanut butter and applesauce.
3. Mix in flax meal and oatmeal.
4. Drizzle the 2 tablespoons of honey and 1 tablespoon of water over the dough and mix with a spoon.
5. Switch to kneading by hand. If dough feels like it's not holding together, add ½ to 1 tablespoon more of water and keep kneading until dough is a stiff, slightly sticky ball.
6. Let dough sit for 20 minutes in the bowl.
7. Roll dough out on wax paper and cut into 1 ½-inch-size treat shapes (or your favorite treat shape).
8. Bake for 15–20 minutes or until bottoms are browned. Once browned, turn oven down to 200° and bake for 10 more minutes.

Blueberry Yummies

BLUEBERRY YUMMIES

Many nutritionists recommend blueberries because they are high in antioxidants. Antioxidants have many roles in the body. They can remove free radicals and can help strengthen the immune system. These treats come out a bluish/purple color, but you can be confident it is from the blueberries and not some artificial additive or preservative. Makes approx. 5 dozen.

Ingredients:
½ C whole blueberries (fresh or frozen; if frozen, thaw and drain excess water)
½ C uncooked oatmeal
1 Tbsp vegetable oil
1 Tbsp honey
¾ C unbleached white flour, divided into ½ C and ¼ C

Directions:
1. Preheat oven to 350°.
2. Put blueberries in a food processor and blend until almost liquid.
3. In a separate bowl, blend oatmeal and ½ cup of flour.
4. Add the blueberry puree to oat mixture and blend.
5. Drizzle the oil and honey on top of the dough and mix until dough comes together in a ball.
6. Flatten the sticky dough in the bowl and work in by hand the remaining ¼ cup of flour.
7. On wax paper, roll out and cut into 1-inch circles (or your favorite small shape) until all dough is used.
8. Bake for 15 minutes or until bottoms are browned. Turn off oven and place treats back in cooling oven for 15–25 minutes to harden.

Beggin' for Bananas

BEGGIN' FOR BANANAS

This treat is low in fat, sodium, and sugar, but ranks high in taste! The aroma of banana and cinnamon will fill your kitchen and invite you and your pet pal to wait by the oven door for these scrumptious goodies to finish baking. Makes approx. 3 dozen.

Ingredients:
1 ripe banana
½ C ground flax meal
1 tsp cinnamon
1 ¼ C uncooked oatmeal, divided into five ¼ C portions
2 Tbsp water
2 Tbsp wheat flour

Directions:
1. Preheat oven to 350°.
2. Peel and mash banana.
3. Blend in cinnamon and ground flax meal.
4. Mix in oats ¼ cup at a time. When adding the last ¼ cup, knead by hand and form dough into a ball.
5. Roll the ball of dough in the 2 tablespoons of wheat flour to make it easier to handle for rolling out.
6. Place dough between two pieces of wax paper, roll out and cut into your favorite treat shape.
7. Bake for about 15 minutes. At the 10-minute mark, check to see if treat bottoms are browning. When bottoms are lightly brown, flip treats over and place back in oven for 15–20 minutes to brown the other side and to cook all the way through.

APPLE FLAX SNAX

The health benefits of flax, oatmeal, and cinnamon are rolled into this one *fantastic* treat! Flax and oatmeal may lower cholesterol, and cinnamon may assist to stabilize blood sugar levels. As a bonus, this treat has loads of fiber to keep your pooch regular. Makes approx. 4 dozen.

Ingredients:
½ C unsweetened applesauce
½ C ground flax meal
½ C uncooked oatmeal
½ C wheat germ
1 tsp cinnamon
2 Tbsp vegetable oil
¾ C unbleached white flour, divided into three ¼ C portions

Directions:
1. Preheat oven to 350°.
2. Evenly blend applesauce, flax, oats, and wheat germ.
3. Add cinnamon and oil and mix well.
4. Add ¼ cup flour and mix with a spoon.
5. Add another ¼ cup flour and knead by hand. Work some, if not all, of the last ¼ cup of flour in until dough feels firm and not sticky.
6. On wax paper or lightly floured surface, roll out dough and cut your favorite cookie shape.
7. Bake for 15 minutes or until bottoms are lightly browned. Once lightly browned, turn off oven and place treats back in cooling oven for 20–25 minutes to harden.

NANNA NUTTERS

Your beloved dog will go *crazy* for the combo of bananas and peanut butter! These are simple to make and quick to bake. A treat so comforting, it will be like a warm hug in your pup's tummy! Makes approx. 3 dozen.

Ingredients:
1 ripe banana
¼ C creamy, unsalted peanut butter
½ C wheat germ
¾–1 C unbleached white flour, divided into four ¼ C portions

Directions:
1. Preheat oven to 325°.
2. Peel and mash the banana, then mix in peanut butter.
3. Blend in wheat germ.
4. Add flour ¼ cup at a time with the same mashing technique like you were mashing the banana.
5. When adding the third ¼ cup portion of flour, begin kneading by hand. Knead the dough until the oil from the peanut butter comes through (it will feel slightly greasy) and form into a ball. Here is where you may *not* need the last ¼ cup of flour if a ball of dough forms after the third addition of flour.
6. Lightly dust the outside of the dough ball with flour and roll out onto wax paper. Cut into your dog's favorite treat shape.
7. Bake 12–18 minutes or until bottoms are lightly browned. Once lightly brown, turn off oven and put treats back in cooling oven for an additional 15 minutes to harden.

Baking Notes:

CHAPTER 4

LIP SMACKIN' GREAT ANYTIME TREATS

No doubt, these are lip smackin' great treats!

MEGAROONI SNACKS

I named this snack in honor of my dog, Meg. It was the first treat inspired during my quest to make healthy alternatives to store-bought treats. With the yummy taste of peanut butter and health benefits of flax (high levels of omega-3 fatty acids and fiber), this one's a winner for all breeds! Makes approx. 4 dozen.

Ingredients:
1 C uncooked oatmeal
1 C wheat flour
¼ C creamy, unsalted peanut butter
½ C ground flax meal
1 Tbsp canola oil
½ cup water

Directions:
1. Preheat oven to 350°.
2. Mix all ingredients *except* the water until well blended together.
3. Add water and stir well.
4. Knead dough by hand until it holds together in a ball.
5. Roll out dough on a lightly floured surface and cut out into favorite treat shape.
6. Bake for 20 minutes or until bottoms are lightly browned. Once lightly browned, turn off oven and leave treats in cooling oven for an additional 30–40 minutes to harden.

Chicken Bones

CHICKEN BONES

This treat *always* gets rave reviews from the dogs! Every "pet parent" will beg to know when they can get some more. See, humans can learn new tricks too! Be sure to keep the sodium content low by using the recommended organic, no- salt-added chicken broth. Makes approx. 5–6 dozen.

Ingredients:
2 ½ C wheat flour
½ C white cornmeal
½ tsp garlic powder (not garlic salt)
1 Tbsp melted butter
1 ¼ C no-salt-added organic chicken broth, divided into 1 C and ¼ C

Directions:
1. Preheat oven to 375°. (See step #7 as well)
2. In a large bowl, combine wheat flour, cornmeal, and garlic powder until evenly distributed.
3. Blend in melted butter and 1 cup of the chicken broth.
4. When dough gets crumbly, begin kneading by hand.
5. Add remaining chicken broth 1–2 tablespoons at a time to monitor the consistency of the dough. If the dough gets too sticky to handle, add a bit more flour.
6. Roll dough out on wax paper or floured surface and cut into a bone (or your favorite) shape.
7. Just when you put the treats in the oven, turn oven temperature down to 325° and bake for 30–40 minutes or until bottoms are browned and treats feel hard to the touch. Note: treats will harden more upon cooling.

Honey Butter Bones

HONEY BUTTER BONES

If your dog loves butter, like mine, then this treat will be an absolute delight! The natural sweetness of honey makes this irresistible to dogs with a bit of a sweet tooth. Makes approx. 2 dozen.

Ingredients:
½ C unbleached, white flour; plus 2–3 Tbsp
½ C wheat germ
2 Tbsp unsalted butter
2 Tbsp honey
3 Tbsp water
½ tsp pure vanilla extract

Directions:
1. Preheat oven to 325°.
2. Blend ½ cup flour with wheat germ until evenly blended.
3. In a separate microwave safe bowl, melt butter.
4. Add honey, vanilla, and water to melted butter. Mix until honey dissolves.
5. Add butter/honey mixture to flour/wheat germ and mix until crumbly.
6. Knead in flour 1 tablespoon at a time until a soft dough forms.
7. Roll out on wax paper and cut into your favorite treat shape.
8. Bake 25–30 minutes or until treats are browned.
9. Once browned, turn off oven and leave treats in cooling oven for 15–20 minutes to harden.

My eye is on this one!
Oats-N-Honey

OATS – N – HONEY

With only four ingredients these are a snap to make! Oats – N – Honey is sure to warm your doggie's tummy. They're so delicious and sweet, it's hard to believe they're such a healthy treat! Makes approx. 2 dozen.

Ingredients:
2 C uncooked oatmeal, divided in half
⅓ C wheat germ
2 Tbsp honey
½ C water, divided in half

Directions:
1. Preheat oven to 350°.
2. Take 1 cup of the oats and blend with all the wheat germ.
3. Add 2 tablespoons of honey and ¼ cup of water and mix well.
4. Add remaining 1 cup oatmeal to dough a little at a time working in by hand. Add remaining water as needed to keep the oats sticking to the dough.
5. On wax paper, roll out dough and cut into your favorite treat shape.
6. Bake for 15–20 minutes or until bottoms are lightly browned. Once lightly browned, turn off oven and leave treats in cooling oven for 20–30 minutes to dry out and harden.

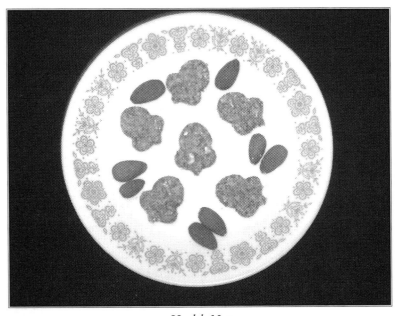

Health Nut

HEALTH NUT

For the health-conscious pet parent, this treat is for you! This has fabulous flavor and is loaded with fiber and heart healthy unsaturated fats (found in almonds and flax meal). Go ahead and try one for yourself—your dog won't tell! Makes approx. 2 dozen.

Ingredients:
30 natural, unsalted almonds
¼ C wheat germ
¼ C uncooked oatmeal
2 Tbsp ground flax meal
⅛ tsp cinnamon
3 Tbsp water
¼ C wheat flour, plus more for dough roll out

Directions:
1. Preheat oven to 350°.
2. Put almonds in a food processor for 30-45 seconds or until almonds are to a coarse flour consistency.
3. In a separate bowl, mix oats, wheat germ, flax, and cinnamon until evenly blended.
4. Add water and almonds. Mix until crumbly.
5. By hand, knead in wheat flour until it is firm dough.
6. On a lightly floured surface, roll dough out and cut out into your favorite treat shape.
7. Bake for 20–25 minutes or until bottoms are browned and treats are hard to the touch. Begin checking treats at the 20-minute mark of the suggested baking time to check for doneness.

I can almost reach my oatmeal cookie!

OATMEAL COOKIE

This is as close to the real deal as a dog can get to an oatmeal cookie! Don't be surprised if the whole family is jealous when you're making these treats. Your kitchen will smell like a yummy batch of oatmeal cookies, and your dog will start doing tricks before these treats are even out of the oven! Makes approx. 2–2 ½ dozen.

Ingredients:
½ C uncooked oats
½ C wheat flour
1 Tbsp sugar
½ tsp cinnamon
3 Tbsp water
2 Tbsp melted, unsalted butter

Directions:
1. Preheat oven to 325°.
2. Mix together oats, flour, sugar, and cinnamon until evenly blended.
3. Add water and melted butter and mix well.
4. Knead by hand until a ball of dough forms.
5. Roll out dough on wax paper and cut out into favorite treat shape.
6. Bake for 25–30 minutes or until bottoms are lightly browned.

Carrot Crunchers are hoppin' healthy

CARROT CRUNCHERS

Many dogs (and humans) *love* carrots. This treat is so tasty the whole family will want to try one! The bonus about carrots is that they are loaded with vitamin A, which may be beneficial for the eyes! Makes approx. 3 ½–4 dozen.

Ingredients:
4-ounce jar organic carrot baby food
1 C brown rice flour, divided in half
½ C wheat flour, plus 2 Tbsp for rolling out
1 Tbsp brown sugar
1 Tbsp canola oil
1 Tbsp honey
½ tsp cinnamon

Directions:
1. Preheat oven to 350°.
2. Blend rice flour with all other ingredients *except* wheat flour until dough is crumbly.
3. Add ½ cup of wheat flour to dough by kneading in by hand until a slightly sticky ball of dough forms.
4. Roll out on wax paper and cut into favorite treat shape. You may have to dust dough lightly after each roll out to prevent sticking to rolling pin.
5. Bake treats on a non-stick cookie sheet for 25–35 minutes or until bottoms are browned. Treats will harden upon cooling.

Baking Notes:

_____

_____

_____

_____

_____

_____

_____

_____

_____

_____

_____

_____

_____

_____

_____

_____

_____

_____

_____

_____

_____

_____

_____

_____

_____

_____

_____

_____

_____

_____

_____

_____

_____

_____

_____

CHAPTER 5

SPOILED ROTTEN TREATS

These are a few of my favorite toys!

PIZZA PUPS

Let's not forget your furry friend on pizza night! These are so quick to make that you can have them done before the pizza man arrives. Your dog will be pawing over these perfect little pizzas! Makes approx. 2 ½ dozen.

Ingredients:
1 C wheat flour
2 Tbsp tomato paste (not sauce)
2 Tbsp grated parmesan cheese
¼ tsp garlic powder (not garlic salt)
¼ tsp dried oregano
1 Tbsp olive oil
¼ C water, plus an extra 1–2 Tbsp

Directions:
1. Preheat oven to 350°.
2. Evenly blend together wheat flour, garlic, oregano, and parmesan cheese.
3. Add tomato paste, oil, and ¼ cup of water.
4. Mix with a spoon until stiff and a bit crumbly.
5. Knead by hand. If the dough is not binding completely together, add another tablespoon of water and continue working by hand until you have a non-sticky ball of dough.
6. Roll out dough on wax paper and cut into a round pizza shape (or your favorite treat shape).
7. Bake for 20–25 minutes until treats are hard and bottoms are brown.

TURKEY BACON BLISS

Reward your pup's visit to the vet with this indulgent treat. All the dogs on the block will be pawing at the door with anticipation for this treat to finish baking! Note: You may want to freeze leftovers in an airtight container due to the meat content in the treat. Makes 2 dozen mini-muffin-size treats.

Ingredients:
¾ C wheat flour
¼ C white cornmeal
¼ C white flour
¼ C wheat germ
3 strips of turkey bacon, cooked until crispy, cooled, and torn into tiny pieces
3 Tbsp vegetable oil
1 egg
⅓ C water

Directions:
1. Preheat oven to 350°.
2. In a large mixing bowl, combine flours, cornmeal, and wheat germ until evenly blended.
3. Add cooked turkey bacon pieces, oil, egg, and water. Mix well until a stiff dough forms.
4. Put roughly a tablespoon of the dough in a mini-muffin pan and press dough down to fill the entire bottom.
5. Bake 25–30 minutes or until the edges of the treats turn brown.

CHEESEBURGER CUTOUTS

Let's face it, dry kibble can get *B-O-R-I-N-G*! This decadent treat is a snap to make and will rate "4 paws" with your pooch—*guaranteed*! Note: You may want to freeze leftovers in an airtight container due to the meat content in the treat. Makes approx. 2 dozen.

Ingredients:
½ C fully cooked and cooled organic ground beef
¼ C shredded cheese (Swiss or cheddar work best)
⅛ tsp garlic powder (not garlic salt)
1 C wheat flour, divided in half
⅓ C water

Directions:
1. Preheat oven to 350°.
2. Mix cooked beef, cheese, and garlic powder together.
3. Add ½ cup of the wheat flour and all the water. Blend well.
4. Knead in by hand the rest of the wheat flour.
5. Roll dough out on wax paper and cut into dog bone shapes (or your favorite treat shape).
6. Bake for 25–30 minutes or until treats are browned.

Cheese Nibbles

CHEESE NIBBLES

Your pampered pooch will instantly become addicted to these tasty treats. They're *soooo* cheesy and *oh so very pleasy.* This makes approx. 5 dozen so there will be plenty to go around for all your dog's friends. They will be very grateful you shared!

Ingredients:
⅔ C uncooked oatmeal
1 ⅔ C unbleached white flour, divided into 1 C and ⅔ C
2 ounces (approx. 1 C) finely shredded Swiss (or your dog's favorite) cheese
2 Tbsp parmesan cheese
⅔ C low-sodium chicken broth
2 Tbsp melted butter
2 Tbsp water

Directions:
1. Preheat oven to 325°.
2. Mix oatmeal and 1 cup of the flour.
3. Add both cheeses and blend well.
4. Add broth, butter, water, and mix.
5. Add last ⅔ cup flour a little bit at a time by kneading in by hand until dough is no longer very sticky.
6. Roll dough out on wax paper and cut into a bone (or your favorite) treat shape.
7. Bake for 30–35 minutes or until bottoms are browned.

Baking Notes:

_____
_____
_____
_____
_____
_____
_____
_____
_____
_____
_____
_____
_____
_____
_____
_____
_____
_____
_____
_____
_____
_____
_____
_____
_____
_____
_____
_____
_____
_____
_____
_____

Baking Notes:

_____